Branch Lines of East

Volume Thr

Firsby to Spilsby

A. J. Ludlam

Published by the
Lincolnshire Wolds Railway Society

LWRS
PUBLICATIONS

Firsby station staff and some of their children stand in front of the imposing station entrance portico in **GNR** days.

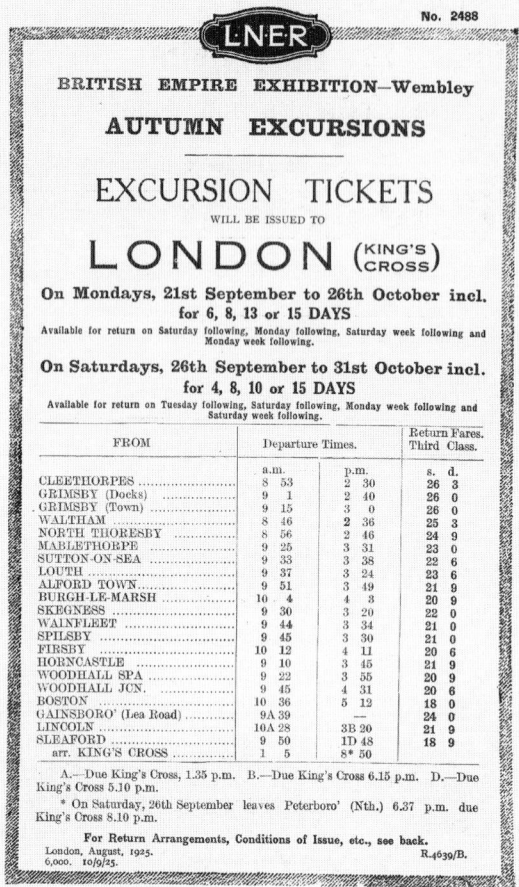

No. 2488

L·N·E·R

BRITISH EMPIRE EXHIBITION—Wembley

AUTUMN EXCURSIONS

EXCURSION TICKETS

WILL BE ISSUED TO

LONDON (KING'S CROSS)

On Mondays, 21st September to 26th October incl.
for 6, 8, 13 or 15 DAYS
Available for return on Saturday following, Monday following, Saturday week following and Monday week following.

On Saturdays, 26th September to 31st October incl.
for 4, 8, 10 or 15 DAYS
Available for return on Tuesday following, Saturday following, Monday week following and Saturday week following.

FROM	Departure Times.		Return Fares. Third Class.	
	a.m.	p.m.	s.	d.
CLEETHORPES	8 53	2 30	26	3
GRIMSBY (Docks)	9 1	2 40	26	0
GRIMSBY (Town)	9 15	3 0	26	0
WALTHAM	8 46	2 36	25	3
NORTH THORESBY	8 56	2 46	24	9
MABLETHORPE	9 25	3 31	23	0
SUTTON-ON-SEA	9 33	3 38	22	6
LOUTH	9 37	3 24	23	6
ALFORD TOWN	9 51	3 49	21	9
BURGH-LE-MARSH	10 4	4 3	20	9
SKEGNESS	9 30	3 20	22	0
WAINFLEET	9 44	3 34	21	0
SPILSBY	9 45	3 30	21	0
FIRSBY	10 12	4 11	20	6
HORNCASTLE	9 10	3 45	21	9
WOODHALL SPA	9 22	3 55	20	9
WOODHALL JCN.	9 45	4 31	20	6
BOSTON	10 36	5 12	18	0
GAINSBRO' (Lea Road)	9A 39	—	24	0
LINCOLN	10A 28	3B 20	21	9
SLEAFORD	9 50	1D 48	18	9
arr. KING'S CROSS	1 5	8* 50		

A.—Due King's Cross, 1.35 p.m.   B.—Due King's Cross 6.15 p.m.   D.—Due King's Cross 5.10 p.m.

* On Saturday, 26th September leaves Peterboro' (Nth.) 6.37 p.m. due King's Cross 8.10 p.m.

For Return Arrangements, Conditions of Issue, etc., see back.

London, August, 1925.
6,000. 10/9/25.
R.4639/B.

ISBN 978-0-9926762-7-8

The Lincolnshire Wolds Railway Society would like to thank Alf Ludlam and Phil Eldridge for giving their time to compile this publication, to Bob Cable, Michael Stewart, Alan Stubbs and Leyland Penn for their contributions and to Allinson Print & Supplies for their support with the project.

Printed by Allinson Print & Supplies, Allinson House, Lincoln Way, Fairfield Industrial Estate, Louth, Lincolnshire LN11 0LS

Issue 1. September 2015.

CONTENTS

A fine display of shiny shoes! Three generations of
the Willis family at Firsby station in November 1963.
Jim Willis (left), his son Walter (second right), who
was a butcher in Spilsby, and grandaughter Barbara.

Celebrating Queen Victoria's Jubilee of 1897 in the Market Place, Spilsby. The statue is of Spilsby's most famous citizen, Sir John Franklin, the explorer.

GNR Class F2 0-4-2 No 110 at Spilsby. Still has its Stirling cab and tender but has an Ivatt domed boiler. Built in 1885 and withdrawn in 1921. The military presence suggests circa 1914.

Spilsby is a small classic market town, situated at the southern edge of the Lincolnshire Wolds. The area around the town has a long history of good mixed farming, the soil is varied, much of it sandy. To the east and south west there is rich loam yielding good crops of wheat, barley, potatoes, beans and mustard. Here too is a rich pastureland, upon which great numbers of sheep and cattle are fattened.

In the town's Market Place stands a bronze statue of Spilsby's most famous son, Sir John Franklin, discoverer of the North West Passage, who died in the Arctic regions in June 1847. There is a memorial to him in Westminster Abbey, with a moving verse written by his nephew, and Lincolnshire's great poet Alfred Lord Tennyson:

"Not here. The White North has thy bones:
and thou
Heroic sailor-soul
Art passing on thine happier voyage now
Toward no earthly pole."

When the railway arrived at Firsby in 1848, there were about 200 people living in the village, a purely agricultural district. Apart from farmers and their workers, Firsby had one shop-keeper cum-beer house keeper, one shoemaker and two corn

GNR 2-2-2T No.33 at Spilsby station in 1869. The station shunting horse and yard crane are clearly seen.

millers. The railway would bring in coal and fertilizers and take out farm produce, with passengers going to Boston Market, as an alternative to a road journey to markets at Spilsby and Wainfleet.

87-year-old May Smith lived at 'The Chestnuts Farm', Firsby. She remembered walking from home with her family to the Methodist Chapel on Sundays three times a day, morning, lunchtime and evening. "Each time we would have to change into our "Sunday Best" and then back into our everyday clothes!" In the summer they would stop and look over the wall of the bridge over the Skegness line to watch trip trains returning home in the evening.

During the war she would cycle to the station during the school holidays and watch the trains coming and going. "I was fascinated by trains, which was quite unusual for a girl. I remember the staff calling out 'this train for Boston, Spalding, Peterborough and London'."

May travelled on the last train on the East Lincolnshire line to Kings Cross, on 4th October, 1970, and still has the ticket. "I will always remember that day – I took my son Danny to visit the Imperial War Museum while we were in London".

A posed photo of Spilsby station in the 1890s which included footplate crew and guard, stationmaster, staff and family and a GNR horse and cart. The train engine is a Sturrock class D 0-4-2 well tank; the coaching stock is comprised of two brake thirds 33ft 10¼in long, the centre coach is No 226, a composite 3,1,1,3,3 35ft 3in long, built in 1881.

A Victorian view of Spilsby station with a good crowd of people on the platform as a 0-4-2 well tank arrives with a passenger train from Firsby.

Plenty of advertising in evidence in this Edwardian view of Spilsby station with 126 class 0-4-2 WT No 122A entering the platform with the goods shed beyond. The signal owed its great height to its need to be seen on the climb into Spilsby station.

Haw's woodyard next to Spilsby station, on the Boston Road, with a 126 class 0-4-2 WT No 122 standing alongside the engine shed.

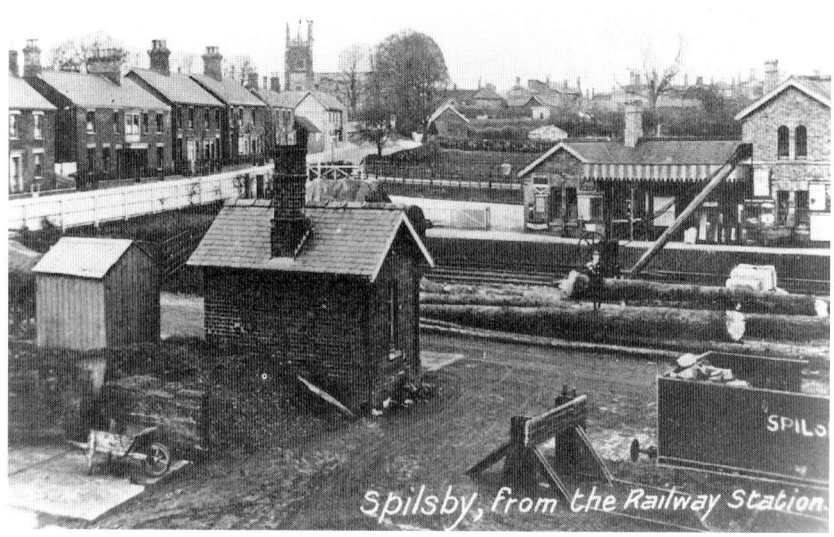

Spilsby station circa 1920 with the weighbridge office in the foreground and Boston Road beyond. Tree trunks for Haw's woodyard are being dealt with by the station crane.

ARRIVAL OF THE RAILWAY - FIRSBY

Firsby station stood in stark contrast to the surrounding area, a solid, impressive, man-made statement, standing in the empty Lincolnshire countryside. The station was designed by Weightman & Hadfield, and built in 1848 as part of the East Lincolnshire Railway (ELR), running between Boston and Grimsby. lt was operated by the Great Northern Railway (GNR), although it remained an independent company until the 1923 grouping.

The importance of Firsby station, and later junction, was determined by its geographical relationship with the important seaport of Wainfleet, four miles to the east and the market town of Spilsby, a corresponding distance to the west. Two independent companies, the Spilsby & Firsby, in 1868 and the Wainfleet & Firsby, in 1871, joined the ELR at Firsby. The latter was extended to Skegness in 1873. By 1880 Skegness had become a popular seaside resort, attracting over 160,000 excursion passengers to the town annually. As all excursion trains from the south had to reverse at the station, the installation of the south curve was deemed essential. The curve was laid double track, and two new signal boxes, Firsby South and Firsby East, were provided. The south curve allowed trains access to the Skegness branch without going into Firsby station.

A fine early photo of the south end of Firsby station in the 1880s. Engine crews, station staff, signal men, platelayers and their families are all present. The engine on the left is bound for Spilsby, the one in the middle for Boston and the one on the right for Skegness.

The impressive entrance to the station was a squat stone arrangement with cornices and a balcony above the arches. The entrance was through a door beneath the portico, which gave on to an L-shaped booking office. To the left was the door to the general waiting room, to the right the ticket office windows, ahead an arch led on to Platform 1.

Once out on Platform 1 there was a strange contradictory feeling of enclosed spaciousness. Above, the steel girder-supported wooden roof threw half its weight on a series of central cast-iron highly decorated arches, an ingenious way of keeping the platforms clear of pillars. Louth and Alford also had this unusual system, although Firsby's was the only one to survive until the closure of the line, in 1970.

Platform 2 had two waiting rooms with coal fires and decorated with poster paintings of a castle in North Wales by Norman Wilkinson and a Yorkshire Dales scene by Frank Sherwin. Platform 3 was unroofed, and a little bleak, and was used by Skegness trains.

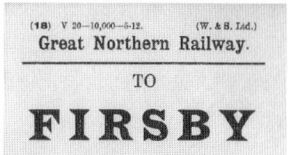

The layout was completed by a brick-built goods shed to the north of the station with superb round-arched windows along its east and west sides. A water tank on a brick-built base and a gas works was alongside Platform 3.

The station remained much the same throughout its life. The station signal box was extended from three to four bays in 1927 to accommodate a larger frame when the east box was closed.

The Cleethorpes, Grimsby and Kings Cross passenger trains that ran through the station in the 1930s were hauled by Ivatt large Atlantic 4-4-2s, lined in LNER green. Nos 4409, 3279, 4429, 4408 and 3282 were all regular performers. Subsequently class B1 4-6-0s worked much of the traffic, until replaced by Britannia Pacifics, which had been displaced from the Great Eastern lines in 1961. They represented a significant increase in power. With the end of steam the smaller Brush Type 2s found the going tough and were replaced by the Brush Type 4s.

93-year-old Harry Thornally worked at J. F. Smith's farm next to Firsby station. "When I first started work I used to take the boss's five year old son on the train to Spilsby on a Saturday to have his hair cut. There was only one return train in the morning and another in the afternoon.

Firsby had its own holding pens that were used for cattle and pigs that were to be transported by rail. We would take about 20 pigs at a time when they were ready for slaughter. The first train in the morning was the mail and newspaper train at around 4.30am. A van would take the mail by road to Spilsby. The first passenger train was the 7.30am from Cleethorpes to Kings Cross, a few passengers would change trains here for the Skegness connection. The morning pick-up goods would shunt the yard, go down to Skegness, then return to Boston. Later in the morning two heavily-loaded iron ore trains, heading for Scunthorpe, would travel slowly through the station. Fish trains bound for London would pass through the station at about 60 mph.

Harry Thornally

On Summer Saturdays trip trains for Skegness would start arriving at about 9.30am. There would be 12 or more up to 11am. Some engines would return to Firsby to be turned on the triangle. Quite often empty stock would be brought back to Firsby and stored on the Spilsby branch because the carriage sidings at Skegness were full.

Freddy Curtis was on his way to work on his BSA 'Bantam' motorcycle. Firsby road gates were closed so he pulled the foot gate open and rode his bike over the track, only to discover that the signalman had locked the foot gate on the other side. The Skegness train came in and took the bike with it, but Freddy survived!

During the war a freight train travelling north was attacked by a German Junkers 88 at Orby crossing, north of Burgh-le-Marsh. The aircraft dropped three bombs, the first missed the train but demolished a farm shed with a cow inside it, the cow was unharmed! The second bomb clipped the engine's tender and landed beside the track but did not explode, the third bomb exploded in a nearby brook."

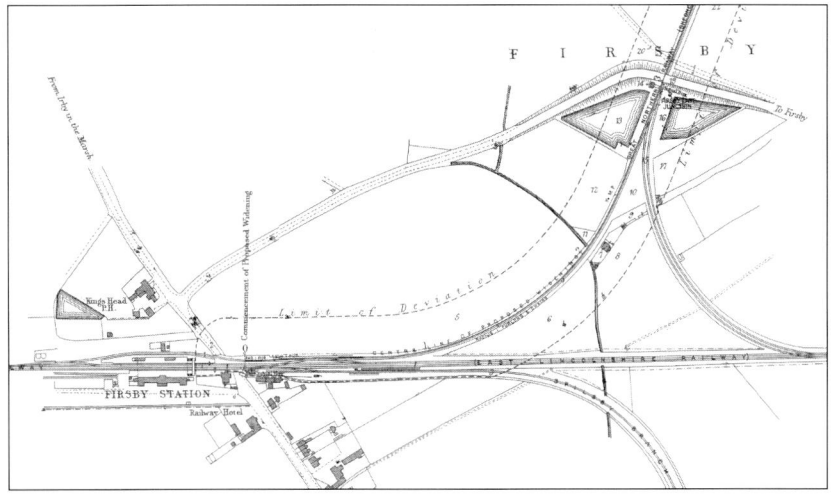

126 class 0-4-2 well tank No 122 seen here on 28th March 1903, rebuilt with an Ivatt domed boiler. Built in 1870 and withdrawn from Boston 1908 and regularly worked over the Spilsby branch. *K. Nunn Collection.*

Class C12 4-4-2T No 4537 with its original "long necked" chimney leaves Firsby station and enters the Spilsby branch with a passenger train in 1936. *J. Kite.*

The Flying Flea

An additional express was introduced in the 1930s, to and from Grimsby, to connect with London expresses at Peterborough. It called at Firsby in the up direction at 8.00 am and at 9.45 pm on the return trip. It began as a train of two coaches, usually hauled by an ex-GCR 4-6-0 from Immingham shed. The tiny train with the big engine was given the title "The Flying Flea", after a small private aircraft that was on the market at the time. It became so popular that by 1939 it had grown into a substantial buffet car express, running right through to Kings Cross, which continued to the end.

Grimsby express fish trains thundered through Firsby station on their journeys to London, the empties returning the next day. In 1920 Nigel Gresley introduced his three-cylindered 2-6-0 fast goods engine, class K3. These were put to work on the fish trains immediately, and virtually monopolised the traffic until their mass withdrawal in 1960/62. Fish duties were taken over by British Railways Standard class 9F 2-10-0s, and, for a brief time in 1963, Britannia Pacifics handled the traffic.

Immingham based class 9F 2-10-0 No 92202 passes through Firsby station and approaches South Junction signal box with a London bound fast fish train on 3rd August 1964. Note the 122 miles from London signpost on the left. *G. Brown.*

A fine panoramic photo of Spilsby station taken from Haw's woodyard. A large Hawthorn 2-2-2 Single No 210 stands in the station. The train is made up of a 3-compartment brake third, No 414; 3-1-4-1-3 coach No 1293, built in 1872 and withdrawn in 1892; 5 compartment all-third No 1647, built in 1875 and withdrawn in 1898 and 3-compartment brake third, built in 1875 and withdrawn in 1891. The coaches were all oil-lit and fitted with two pipe vacuum brakes. Footplate crew, the guard and station staff are in evidence, so too the omnibus for the White Hart Hotel and a GNR wagon and horse. The private-owner wagons in the foreground add a fine touch.

GNR class 126 0-4-2 well tank No 126 at Spilsby station. The first of the class, it was built in November 1868 and withdrawn in June 1907. We have the footplate crew and guard plus the stationmaster and his staff in this fine photo.

Fireman G. H. Luff with class C12 4-4-2T No 4502 at Firsby before working the Spilsby branch in the 1930s.

ARRIVAL OF THE RAILWAY - SPILSBY

By the early 1860s it was felt that Spilsby had suffered compared with other market towns in the area by not having a railway connection. It had lost much of its fatstock market to Burgh-le-Marsh after the opening of the ELR in 1848. A meeting was convened at Spilsby Town Hall on 31st October, 1864. It unanimously carried a resolution, proposed by the Reverend W. V. Turner, that a railway be constructed from Spilsby to a junction with the ELR at Firsby station.

Mr Mackinder moved the resolution that share subscriptions should be taken up immediately, although he indicated that his own stake would be very small.

The Parliamentary agent, Mr Sudlow, estimated the cost of the line would be no more than £5,000 per mile, and that the greatest profits would be savings on the cost of carrying coal, corn, cattle cake and other essential articles.

An agreement was finalised with the GNR in April, 1865 for that company to operate the line, paying the Spilsby & Firsby 40% of the gross receipts. It would operate the line for twenty-one years providing rolling stock and staff, the Spilsby & Firsby company being responsible for the construction works.

The line was Authorised by Parliament on 5th July, 1865. After an initial enthusiasm, the take-up of shares almost reached a standstill, and, by June 1866,

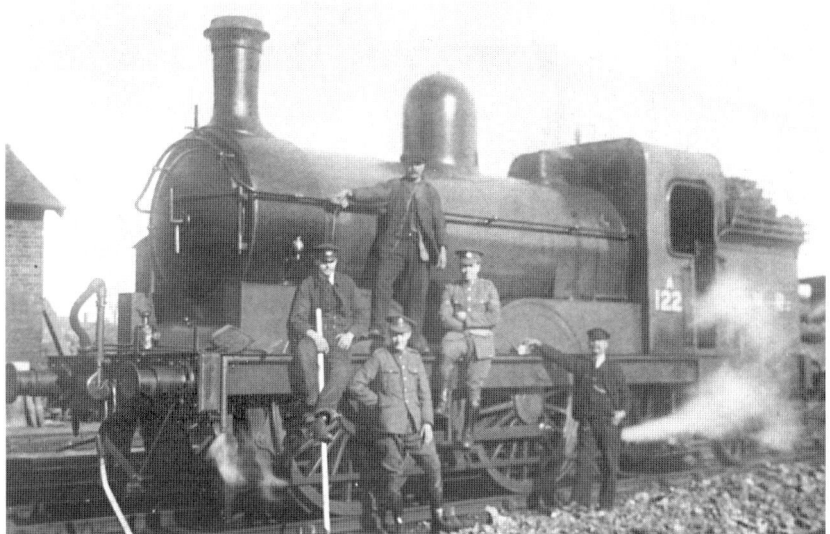

A 126 class 0-4-2 WT No 122 as rebuilt with a 4'5" diameter Ivatt domed boiler at Spilsby, the engine crew and a shunter accompanied by two men in uniform.

when construction work should have begun, much share capital remained to be acquired. Work on the construction of the branch finally began in March 1867, but even then the future was by no means certain.

Work progressed quickly and the track reached Firsby in August 1867. The Board of Trade Inspector, Captain Tyler, visited the railway in April 1868 suggesting a few alterations. These were carried out and the line opened on 1st May, 1868. The minute book of the old George Inn Club noted for its entry for 1st May, 1868:

"The day was beautifully fine and great crowds of people came to the town. The church bells rang all day (!) Flags and bunting waved in the breeze. At 12.40 pm an official train started, full of passengers, for Firsby, and returned at 1.30 pm. A public luncheon was held in the Town Hall, 120 attended. Mander's Menageries and other exhibits were in town and helped to complete a very successful day".

The Spilsby branch was 4 miles 14 chains in length. Spilsby had a goods shed, an engine shed and cattle pens, but no signal box. Staff at Spilsby consisted of the stationmaster, two porters, two clerks, one man in the goods shed, one man in the yard to wash out the cattle dock, plus other duties and one man delivering and collecting by horse and dray, later a motor lorry. The White Hart horse-drawn bus worked between the station and the town, driven by Mr E. Relph.

Spilsby station from Boston Road in July 1950. A cattle wagon stands in the foreground, so too the yard crane. Beyond is the goods shed, the round-topped building was a fuel store. *M. Black.*

Class C12 4-4-2T No 67350 with the daily goods to Spilsby on 28th July 1952. A platelayers trolley stands alongside a half mile marker post. No 67350 was the first of a class of 60 engines which became very familiar in Lincolnshire over the years. *J. Culpit.*

Class J6 0-6-0 No 64227 in the charge of driver R. Craig and fireman Harry Bonus with the daily goods at Spilsby in October 1958. The goods shed is beyond the locomotive. *M. Black.*

A visit by the Railway Travel and Correspondence Society to Spilsby on 16th May 1954 with class J6 0-6-0 No 64199 in charge. The notice over the flag reads "Spilsby welcomes the Railway Correspondence & Travel Society". *H. B. Priestly.*

The 3.45 pm arrival from Spilsby passes Firsby station signal box and enters the station. Driver Barwick looks out of the cab of class C12 4-4-2T No 4537 in 1936. *G. Brown.*

The Spilsby engine and brake van in the down sidings at Firsby in early February 1948, taken from the end of the platform. Class C12 4-4-2T No E7387, must have been one of the first of Doncaster's British Railways repaint jobs. The 'E' prefix was used for six weeks only during February and March of that year, before the decision was taken to add 60,000 to ex-LNER numbers. *G. Brown.*

SPILSBY ENGINE SHED

The locomotive shed at Spilsby was situated, unusually, in the centre of the sidings in the southern half of the yard. The southernmost of these sidings, was, for the most of its length, private. Originally it had served both the oil storage tanks and a flour and animal feed mill. This unsatisfactory arrangement ceased in the 1940s, with the building of a new petrol storage depot on the north side of the terminus, to cater for the increasing needs of local farmers who were changing over from horses to tractors.

The engine shed was large enough to house a tank engine. Occupying part of the roof was a water tank. This was for domestic purposes, other than drinking water. Water was drawn from a well under the shed, "lift" being by a device similar to a locomotive injector, steam for the operation being supplied by the engine's steam heating pipe. It took two hours to raise one foot of water in the tank, with a steam pressure of 40 psi. Drinking water was supplied by the well, but raised by hand-pump. During the 1950s the engine shed was demolished, having become redundant after the demise of passenger traffic in 1939.

The east end of the station layout at Spilsby in the 1950s, the engine shed to the left and the goods shed to the right with the station beyond.

Class J6 0-6-0 No 64214 stands near the goods shed at Spilsby with the daily goods train on the 22nd November 1958. *H. Davis.*

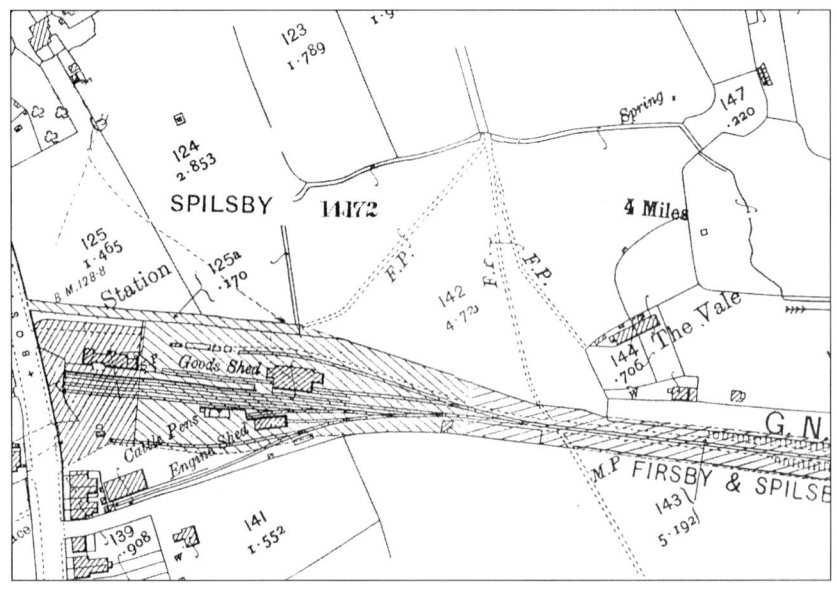

Spilsby Church

The Avenue

Spilsby

Spilsby

Spilsby

SPILSBY

Wish you were here...

Two early postcards extol the virtues of Spilsby and Halton Holgate.

G. N. R.
Series B.
Series B
6064
SPILSBY
SPILSBY to
SPILSBY
KING'S CROSS, LONDON
KING'S CROSS
KING'S CROSS
Fare 10s.6d. Third Class Fare 10s.6d.
SEE CONDITIONS ON BACK
6064

ALES

HALTON HOLGATE, SPILSBY.

Boston-bound dmu at Firsby on Saturday 5th September, 1970. *B. Cable.*

A dmu stands at Platform 3, the Skegness platform at Firsby. The imposing water tank that once stood to the right of the train has long since gone. *B. Cable.*

A Boston-bound dmu leaves Firsby station. *B. Cable.*

L. N. H. R.

Series B   Series B

6172

FIRSBY   FIRSBY

FIRSBY to

LOUTH

LOUTH   LOUTH

Fare 2s.4d.   Third Class   Fare 2s.4d.

SEE CONDITIONS ON BACK

Firsby Station Foreman Ron Thornley helps a passenger alight from a Cleethorpes-Kings Cross train on the last weekend before closure of the East Lincolnshire line. *R. Thornley.*

L.N.E.R. (Series B)

Not transferable. This ticket is issued subject to the notices & conditions in the Company's current time tables. AVAILABLE ON DAY OF ISSUE ONLY

5414

HALTON HOLGATE to
FIRSBY

Fare / S / 4d.
THIRD / 271 / CLASS
FIRSBY

5414

Halton Holgate station today. The building retains its original character, except for the addition of the conservatory which stands on the trackbed of the branch. The goods shed is visible in the background. *P. Eldridge.*

The lovingly-restored 'Barton's Halt' - formerly the railway gatehouse at Granny Barton's Crossing, between Firsby and Halton Holgate. *P. Eldridge.*

24

The Effect of the Railway on the Town

Although the arrival of the railway in Spilsby was late, it made a significant impact on the life of the town. There were many who would claim that not only the Spilsby markets and fairs, but also the Partney sheep and lamb fairs had received an important boost by the arrival of the railway.

However, there was a downside. The accessibility of the shoe factories of Northampton and Leicester saw the end of the trade in Spilsby. The woodworking trade shrunk, and, in 1900, only two or three men were still making the "Spilsby chair". Barrat's rope-making factory closed in 1910 and Spilsby Brewery in 1914, its beers and stouts having previously been judged "entirely free from Arsenic and other poisonous ingredients". The Hundleby brickworks succumbed to the better products of the Peterborough brick kilns.

This was an era of great change, whereas some tradesmen suffered others prospered. Leslie Dodds, an ironmonger, moved into car sales and repairs. J. K. Spence, another ironmonger, sold all popular makes of bicycles and even made his own "Eresby" bicycle.

Throughout the country many hundreds of small towns, like Spilsby, witnessed the death of local crafts and trades and the birth of improvements in transport and the industrialisation and specialisation of the new age.

Today Spilsby is an energetic small town, retaining much of it its rural character.

Fireman G. H. Luff relaxes on the platform at Spilsby before his class C12 engine works a passenger train back to Firsby in the 1930s.

Halton Holgate station seen from the road overbridge in June 1950. A couple of wagons stand outside the goods shed and the station still retains its canopy. *M. Black.*

Class J6 0-6-0 No 64214 enters Halton Holgate station with a daily goods train bound for Spilsby on 22nd November 1958. The station has lost its canopy and running-in board. *H. Davies.*

HALTON HOLGATE

Halton Holgate is a village between Spilsby and the River Lymn, it looks across the Fens to Boston Stump, 15 miles away. This was the only intermediate station on the Spilsby branch. The station had a stationmaster, two porters, four platelayers, a person in charge of Peasgate gatehouse and someone at Little Steeping crossing.

In the 1920s Walter Hickman moved to Halton Holgate from the Spalding area. He brought with him farming methods from that region. He set fruit trees in rows, about twenty yards apart, between them he set thousands of spring flowering bulbs. In another field he set out blackcurrant bushes, strawberry plants and peas.

His establishment created a lot of work at fruit and flower gathering times. Ernest Borrill recalled his mother going strawberry picking between 4.00 and 7.00 am, at which time she would return home to get the children their breakfast and off to school. She was back in the fields at 9.00 am, returning home at midday to get her husband and children their dinner, before returning to the fields until 5.00 pm. Her rate of pay was 6d (2½p) an hour. The fruit and vegetables were loaded onto the train at Halton Holgate station at 9.40 am, transferred to the London train at Firsby, and reached London at 12.25 pm.

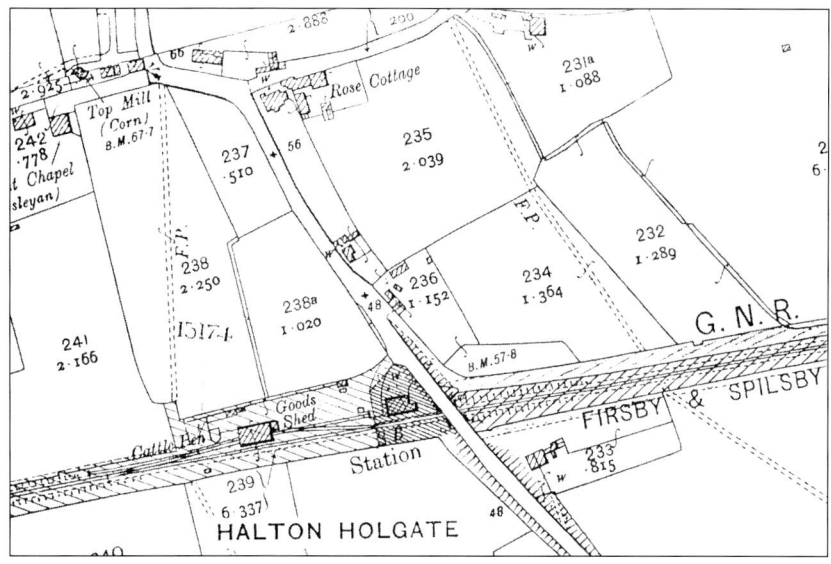

Joe Shaw, the butcher at Halton Holgate, would take the train to Boston on Wednesday morning and return on the 4.30 pm. At the rear of the trains was a cattle wagon containing a bullock. The wagon was shunted off at Halton Holgate and the beast driven up to the Shaw's premises. The family would sit down and eat their meal and afterwards slaughter the beast. It was sold on the rounds on Friday and Saturday, no freezers in those days.

The sidings at Halton Holgate ran east to west, through the goods shed. On the west side of the shed was the cattle dock, to the south east the place where the coal and general goods were unloaded. At this point the line ran slightly uphill, east to west. Shunting wagons off the train was easy, they were shunted off downhill, the porter using a shunting pole to lever the brake tight-on at the stopping place.

Getting wagons out of the siding was a different procedure and involved using a wire cable. Because of the danger of fire the locomotive was not allowed through the goods shed and so the cable was attached to it as it stood on the main line. The other end was hooked onto the waiting wagons and the engine pulled hard and quickly towards the west and as the wagons got level with the goods shed the cable was released and the wagons passed through the shed with their own momentum - a rather dangerous movement, but interesting to watch. The brake was applied to stop the wagons rolling back, the locomotive reconnected and continued to Spilsby.

The idylic looking Halton Holgate station looking towards Firsby in June 1950. The station retains its canopy, running-in board and gentlemen's toilet sign. A lamp stands alongside the lever-controlled access to the goods yard and shed. *M. Black.*

A former three-arm signal at Firsby station reduced to a two arm. The lower arm replaced by a banner following the closure of the Spilsby branch. The top arm is off for the departure of a train over the through-road to Skegness. The second arm dealt with the departure of trains to Boston, a regular occurance every Wednesday at about 8.40 was when the Spilsby branch engine to be relieved took out the Boston market train. *G. Brown.*

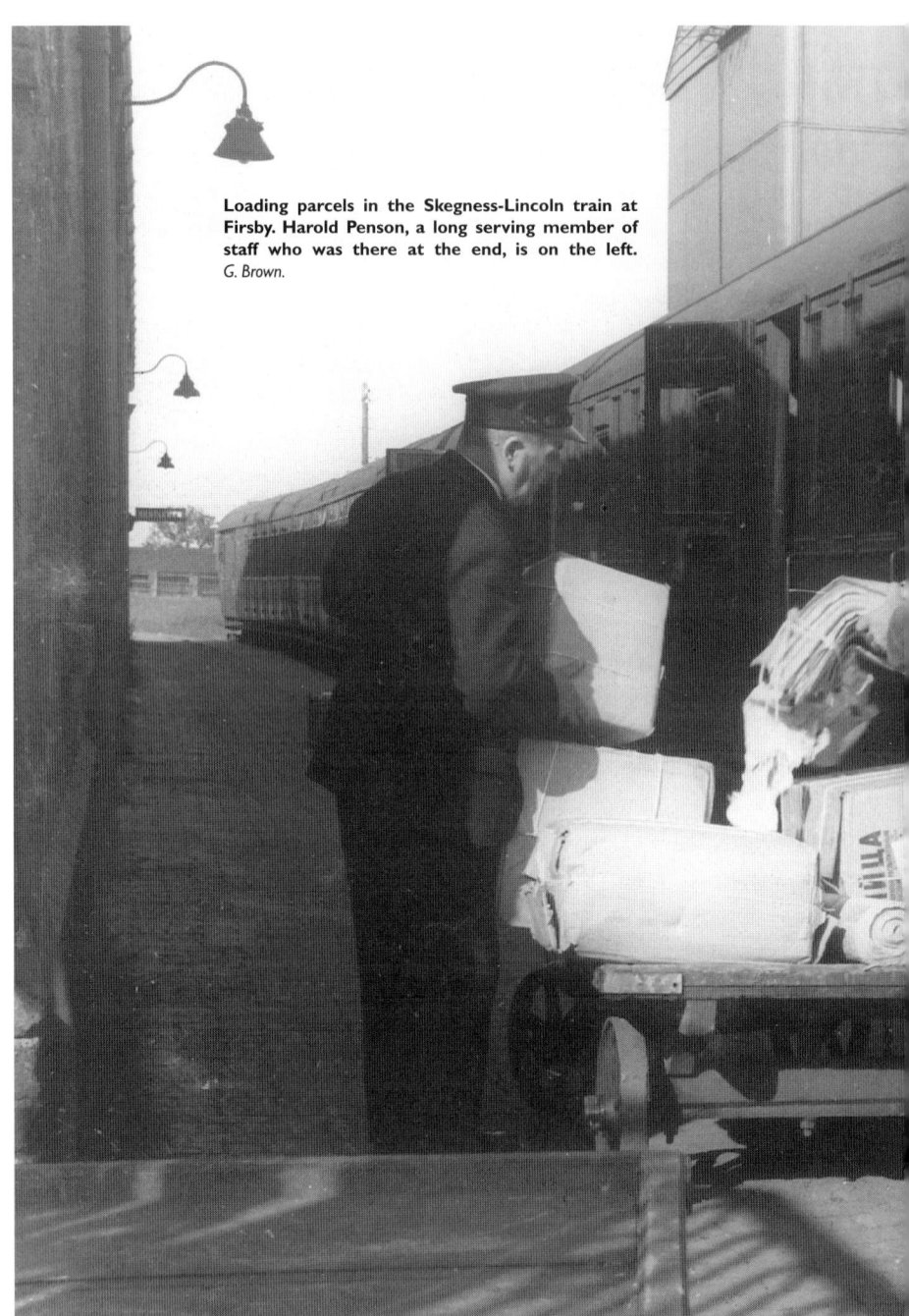

Loading parcels in the Skegness-Lincoln train at Firsby. Harold Penson, a long serving member of staff who was there at the end, is on the left.
G. Brown.

Class B1 4-6-0 No 61240 "Harry Hinchcliffe" passes Firsby East signal box light engine, having been turned on the triangle on 1st July 1964. *G. Brown.*

H. A. Ivatt carried out trials with four-cylinder compounds Nos 292 and 1300 resulting in reduced coal consumption. His third, and last, attempt at compounding was No 1421 (later 4421) built in 1907. Its more economical running was offset by various mechanical problems. Gresley made some modifications in 1913/14. Owing to a badly cracked main frame it entered Doncaster works in March 1920 and was rebuilt as a two cylinder Atlantic which survived until August 1947. Seen here with a passenger train at Firsby in 1945. *T. G. Hepburn.*

THE LINE AT WORK

On the May Day Holiday of 1868, a thousand people travelled to Spilsby by rail. In May of that year a total of 1,863 passengers were booked from Spilsby, in June 1,042 and in July 1,633. However, it was ten years after the opening before the company declared a dividend on ordinary shares, most of the profits of the previous years went to pay off the company's liabilities. Between 1882 and 1885 a dividend of 4% was paid. Up to this point traffic receipts had increased in real terms, but from 1885 to 1888 they dropped disastrously, and, in spite of levelling out, the company was crippled beyond recovery. On 29th April, 1889 an extraordinary meeting agreed to sell the company to the GNR for £8 per share. The GNR paid £20,000 and the take-over was authorised by an Act of 25th July, 1890, to take effect from 1st January, 1891.

Most people in the district used to kill a pig for bacon and needed salt for curing the meat. This would be delivered to Spilsby station and the load split between Mr Lake of Spilsby and Mr Borrill of Halton Holgate. The salt was stored over the brick baking oven, where it soon hardened and was delivered, wrapped in newspaper, by the bread cart on its normal rounds.

Flour and offal was delivered by rail until the General Strike in 1926, after which road transport began deliveries. The ten stone sacks were stood up and pushed onto a running barrow, crossed the goods shed and were loaded onto a wagon waiting near the door. If the flour was delivered by box van, it could be unloaded by hand. If it arrived in open wagons it meant that the sacks were loaded one on top of the other which made unloading difficult.

One of the worst things to handle was linseed and cotton seed cakes for cattle. These were thin cakes, about 36 inches by 12 inches and 1 inch thick, always packed tight in the far ends of the wagons, lying on their sides. They would weigh about 200 cakes to the ton and cotton seed about 175 cakes to the ton. The cakes were packed in threes, in wet weather it was a job keeping them dry.

The engines that worked the branch were supplied by Boston shed. The changeover of engines took place on Wednesdays, the new engine worked down with empty stock and the old engine returned to Boston on the 9.00 am market special.

No 33A, built by Sharp, Roberts & Co. for the GNR, and later rebuilt as a tank engine by Sturrock, worked the first train over the branch. There is a photograph of a large Hawthorn 2-2-2 single at Spilsby, but by and large the branch was worked by tank engines. By the mid-1890s 0-4-2 well tanks were much in evidence on the line. Two Stirling 5ft 6in 0-4-4Ts Nos 118A and 122A were at work over the branch, other 0-4-4-Ts at Boston were numbered 515, 941 and 943, all of which no doubt worked the Spilsby line.

With the arrival of the Ivatt class C12 4-4-2Ts at Boston in 1921, the majority of the work on the line was carried out by these engines, usually numbers 4502 (later 7360), 4504 (7362) and 4009A (7350).

The duties of the branch engines were working of passenger trains, the working of freight traffic and shunting at Spilsby, Halton Holgate and Firsby stations. Running time between Firsby and Spilsby was about ten minutes, and, because of the rising gradient between Halton Holgate and Spilsby, the maximum load was "equal to 18 wagons". Two mixed trains were required in that direction, compared with one in the opposite direction. There was quite a tight curve approaching the incline, a check rail running round it. This meant that tank engines could negotiate the curve and gradient easier than the longer tender engines which tended to bind on the curve.

The GNR Appendix No 4 of 1912 states: "Spilsby branch. Only one engine in steam, or two engines coupled (which will be treated as one engine) allowed on the

An Immingham class K3 2-6-0 No 1838 thunders through Firsby station with an up fish train from Grimsby in 1947. The original station name board can be seen, there was a similar board on the opposite end of the down platform. Both were later replaced by BR tin signs bearing the legend 'Firsby' which were in place by 1957. *G. Brown.*

branch at one time, except in the case of an accident as provided in the general rules and regulations. All points connecting the siding with the running line are secured by a lock, the key of which is the single line train staff".

Bill Copley, who was a fireman from 1928 until the withdrawal of the passenger service in 1939, described the rostering system. "The footplate staff consisted of one driver, one passed fireman, one fireman and one passed cleaner. The times of duty for the driver and passed fireman were at 7.35 am and 12.05 pm respectively. The fireman and passed cleaner had 3.25 am and 3.30 pm turns. The fireman on the 3.25 am turn would book on, light the fire and raise steam. On Mondays, Wednesdays and Fridays his duties would include washing out the boiler, before lighting up. Frequent washing out was necessary because of the use of untreated water. The man who was to drive booked on at 7.35 am ready to begin the service, with the first passenger train to Firsby at 8.05 am. The second driver booked on at 12.05 pm and relieved the first driver for a twenty minute meal-break. After this the 3.25 am man signed off, the passed fireman taking over his firing duties. At 3.30 pm the fourth man would book on for firing duties, the first driver signing off. The 12.05 pm man would assume driving duties. After the last train had run the 12.02 pm man would book off, leaving the 3.30 pm man to throw out the fire, coal and clean the engine."

Carriage washing in the Skegness platform at Firsby. The train most likely to be the Skegness local, which arrived about 4 o'clock to meet up with the local to Boston. At the far end is the class C4 4-4-2 which brought the train in, snow is in evidence in the foreground in this March 1947 shot. *G. Brown.*

Class B1 4-6-0 No 61070 with the 1.50 pm down local passing the goods shed at Firsby with its ornate windows on 2nd September 1963. *G. Brown.*

Before going on duty at East box the relief signalman operates the level crossing gates wheel while Mr Moore deals with a train leaving the down platform for Skegness on Tuesday 4th August 1964. *G. Brown.*

PARTNEY SHEEP AND LAMB FAIRS

On the occasion of the Partney Sheep and Lamb Fairs, sheep were driven in flocks the two miles from Partney to Spilsby station. Tom Kirkham, who worked as a guard on the line for many years, said that sometimes as many as 4,000 animals were gathered at Spilsby station. Once at the station the sheep had to be got into the cattle loading dock and from there into the waiting wagons. About thirty sheep went into each wagon. As one can imagine this kind of work was often somewhat chaotic. The transport of sheep lasted well into LNER days. The working timetable instructions issued by the GNR and dated Sunday 17th - Saturday 23rd September 1911, gives the following instructions: "Monday 18th September, Partney Sheep Fair. The following staff to assist at Spilsby for the day - Guard Wallbanks, Boston Goods; Guard Swain, Boston Goods; Superintendent Shepherd, Boston Goods; Horse Shunter Key, Burgh-le-Marsh. Engines to leave Boston at 10.30 am and 3.30 pm for Firsby to work stock specials as necessary. Last special may be expected to convey stock for the North Eastern Railway line via Barkston. All stock for the NER line will be loaded in dual-piped oil-box wagons. Mr Porcher, Boston, to send guard to Firsby with each engine."

Firsby North signal box and goods shed with the station beyond on 28th March 1967. Notice the grounded Gresley coach, used as a mess hut. *H. B. Priestley.*

37

Class J11 0-6-0 No 4305 at the down platform at Firsby in 1947. It has either come from or about to depart for Skegnesss as the main crossover is set. The Spilsby line and its safety neck is visible beyond the signal box, so too its upper quadrant signal, changed from a somersault in the early 1930s. *G. Brown.*

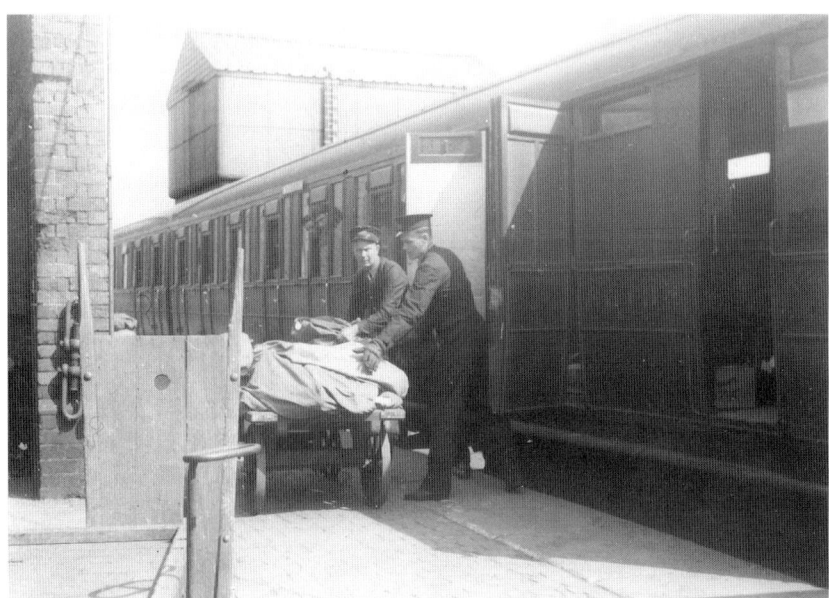

Loading mail in the Skegness platform at Firsby, the water tank at the side of the train. The small roof board on the train is lettered "Skegness". Facing is Mr Dickson, a long serving member of staff, helped by Mr Duncan in 1947. *G. Brown.*

PLATELAYERS

A four-man platelaying gang took care of the maintenance of the branch, their home station was Halton Holgate. In the 1950s the gang was made up of: ganger Bill Rinson, Cyril Turner, Harry Tomblin and Edward Borrill. The main platelayers hut was across the line from Halton Holgate goods shed. It was built of sleepers and comprised of two sections, one for tools and the inner one, a comfortable compartment which had wooden bench seats down each side and a fire grate at the far end. On the wall was a cupboard in which the ganger kept timesheets, detonators and rule books, which, on wet days, the men were supposed to read and learn. Keeping the hut clean and tidy and lighting fires was the job of the last man to join the gang. Fires were not lit with paper but with "churlies", a stick of wood sliced wafer thin several times along its length but remaining joined at the base.

The track was mainly ballast laid on soil, and in the wet season this meant an abundance of weeds, it was virtually impossible to keep the length clear weeding by hand. In June 1957 British Railways (BR) supplied a 40 gallon barrel of weedkiller and a hand pump, which had two pipes with spray nozzles attached. The two halves of a 40 gallon barrel were filled with weed killer and put on the trolley. One man pushed the trolley, a second man rode on the trolley operating the pump, while two men walked alongside spraying each side of the tracks and overlapping in the middle. The spray was a great success and regarded as a "Godsend".

The length of most of the rails on the branch were 21 ft, the weight of the track varied from 85 lbs to 98 lb lengths. The shortness of the rail lengths meant correspondingly more fishplates to undo, scrape clear, oil and replace. Spot sleepering was carried out with good, but not new sleepers. In Spilsby yard the weight of the trains used to force the clay up between the sleepers, the clay had to be dug out and replaced by ballast regularly. A constant problem for the platelayers in the latter days was the river bridge half-a-mile east of Halton Holgate station, which had started to collapse. The walls had been shored-up with 9 inch timbers three feet above the water, and with the walls of the bridge sinking keeping the line level over it was a regular job. The bridge was constructed of two main steel girders and a floor. The men used shims of various thickness under the chairs to level up the line. In the end the bridge was to prove a major factor in the closure of the line.

Firsby station and signal box looking south on 25th May 1970. The Skegness line joins the main Boston to Grimsby line from the left, the entrance to the Spilsby branch can be seen beyond the buffer stop near the signal box. The unusual overlapping crossing gates are seen to good advantage. *G. Brown.*

Class J39 0-6-0 No 64823 with the last train on the Spilsby branch on Saturday 30th November 1958 with station staff and footplate crew on view.

Class J6 0-6-0 No 64199 runs around its trains for the return trip from Spilsby to Firsby on 16th May 1954. Members of the RCTS inspect the area near the engine shed.

42

Closure

The branch closed to passengers on 10th September, 1939, the service "suspended", presumably for the duration of the war. The closure prompted the headmaster of Spilsby Grammar School, Mr. Nesbitt, under the pen name "Topi" to include the following lament in the school magazine "The Spilsbian" in December, 1939:

"Oh friendly little Spilsby train
Will no prayers bring you back again?
A cry goes up, a sound of weeping
From Halton Holgate to Little Steeping,
Wringing his hands our Mr Saggers
On his deserted platform staggers
And engine driver Barwick weeps
As carriageless his engine creeps
We'll never know a Road Car bus
That will shunt back and wait for us.
No morning bus by chance or fate
Habitually ten minutes late,
(While the rate of our gait up Boston Road
Could never by the staff be knowed.)
Worse, if to school a wheel we get

One can't do prep a bicyclette,
The sixth form can't do 4B's Latin
With no plush carriage to be sat in.
When shall we next that smell inhale?
Hear the euphonious whistle wail?
Or feel the rich luxurious motion
Like a tub on a stormy ocean?
When next behold those windows clear
Those views of Yarmouth grown so dear?
Those baggage racks where t'was our joy
To hoist some luckless smaller boy?
Oh tempora! Oh mores! Woe!
Let us unman the Maginot-
Let Hitler have the Spanish Main
But give us back our Spilsby train."

Freight continued to be carried on the line until 1958. A report in the "Lincolnshire Standard", on 12th September, 1958, stated: "Rumours, which have been current in Spilsby for some time, of the proposed closure of the branch railway between Spilsby and Firsby have been confirmed this week by a letter from the British Transport Commission. The letter stated that in view of the heavy expenditure necessary in connection with the reconstruction of the under line bridge it is proposed to close the line. The under line bridge is in urgent need of reconstruction at a cost of about £20,000. Struts were placed under the bridge more than two years ago and the River Board have been pressing for their removal as they tend to create blockages in the channel, which causes considerable flooding. In view of the small amount of traffic now being dealt with on the branch closure has been considered and the conclusion reached that the line is unremunerative.

Expenditure of £20,000 on the bridge is not therefore justified and it is proposed to close the branch completely. The matter is very urgent since if the line remains open for a period longer than two or three months, it would be necessary to incur a cost of about £1,000 placing additional struts under the bridge."

Closure was the outcome, despite opposition from Spilsby Parish Council and a challenge from Mr A. Sylvester of the Transport Commission's estimate of £20,000 to reconstruct the bridge over the Steeping River. He wondered if they were mixing up Tennyson's Brook with the Humber or the Forth as the figure was fantastic, he asked how the figure had been arrived at.

Class J39 0-6-0 No 64823 of Boston was the last locomotive to run over the branch, on Saturday 30th November, 1958, the line officially closing the next day. Among those present were Firsby stationmaster Mr Britain, Mr S. Vernon, the last man in charge at Spilsby station, Mr Thacker, the station's last porter and J. W. Leedham, the station lorry driver for many years.

Class B1 4-6-0 No 61188 returning to Derby Friargate with the 1.30 pm from Mablethorpe, passes a field of Lincoln Reds belonging to J. F. Smith on 1st August 1964. Wagons are parked on the Spilsby branch line behind the signal. *G. Brown.*

Ex LMS class 5MT 2-6-0 No 42813 with a trip train at the South Junction, Firsby. The bracket somersault signal was made up of wooden arms on a lattice structure.

Left to right: Firsby Station Foreman Ron Thornley with Porters Albert Skinner and Fred Richardson.

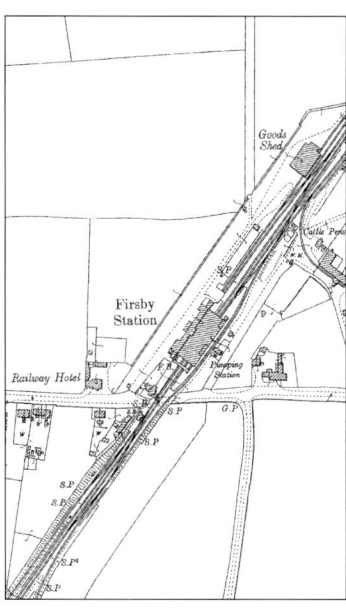

A Skegness bound train leaves Firsby, leaving a Boston bound dmu standing in the station in the late 1960s.

Immingham based Standard "Britannia" Class 4-6-2 No 70038 "Robin Hood" working the morning Cleethorpes-Kings Cross train through Firsby station on 8th August 1962. The remains of the Spilsby line curves away behind the permanent way hut, it extended as far as Granny Barton's crossing. *G. Brown.*

A Right Royal Ending

From 5th May, 1958 the branch was to be served by only one train a day. By October it had spread through the railway grapevine that the line was to close, but before that happened an important event was to take place on the doomed line. Ernest Borrill's diary tells the story:

"November 17: We are getting the track ready for a Royal Train. We were sent an Allen scythe to cut off any tufts of grass showing. The only time anybody would be able to see anything would be for about half-an-hour in the morning.

November 18: We had to rake out and freshen up the cesses at the side of the track for about half-a-mile up to Mrs Barton's crossing.

November 19: We now know that Prince Philip is going to be on the Royal Train. We had to go on duty at 1.30 am. We had a good fire in the lengthman's hut, near where the train was to stop. Four policemen arrived, and, at 2.30 am a darkened train crept out of Firsby station. Harry Tomblin stood near Granny Barton's crossing with a red lamp to stop the train in the right place. After the train came to a standstill we had to place big 3ft 6in square tins between the rails under the train. These caught all the waste from the sinks, hand basins and toilets.

When it began to get daylight at about 7.48 am Firsby stationmaster, Mr Britain, brought the morning papers to the train. The engine was a beautifully clean class B1, steaming but not making a noise, it had been heating the train all night. At 8.10 am we were ordered to remove the tins from under the train and empty them into a hole we had dug. The train moved off slowly taking Prince Philip to inspect a rocket site at North Cotes. We signed off at 9.30 am, this is the only time I shall serve a Royal Train".

The spur of the branch that had been used by the Royal Train remained in place until the late 1960s, used as a wagon siding. Of the stations on the branch Halton Holgate and its goods shed survive, well maintained. At Spilsby the yellow brick station buildings were demolished in 1965. The goods shed, modernised and used for industrial purposes, bears a plaque proclaiming its railway origin.

The 12.42 pm ex-Mablethorpe for Nottingham Victoria, arrival time 2.21 pm, with class B1 4-6-0 No 61390 in charge at Firsby South Junction on Saturday 1st August 1964. Note the long line of wagons parked on the remains of the Spilsby branch. *G. Brown.*

The impressive frontage to Firsby station looking south on 24th May 1970. Notice the wooden supports alongside the portico. *G. Brown.*